Soap Making for Beginners:

Guide to Making Natural Homemade Soaps that will Refresh, Revitalize, and Rejuvenate your Skin

Maurice Wilkinson

All Rights Reserved. No part of this publication may be reproduced in any form or by any means, including scanning, photocopying, or otherwise without prior written permission of the copyright holder. Copyright © 2014

Table of Contents

Chapter 1 – Where Do I Begin and Why Should I Begin?

Chapter 2 – How Do I Do It?

Chapter 3 – Safety First

Chapter 4 – Starting From Scratch

Chapter 5 – This is Not Your Granny's Lye Soap

Chapter 6 – Recipes Soaps That Will Revitalize Your Skin

Chapter 7 – Sweet Smell of Success

Chapter 8 – Resources

Chapter 1 – Where Do I Begin and Why Should I Begin?

Congratulations for picking up "Soap Making for Beginners: Guide to Making Natural Homemade Soaps that will Refresh, Revitalize, and Rejuvenate your Skin." I imagine you have a lot of questions right now and I hope to answer all of them in the next few pages. Most importantly, I want to assure you that you've taken a great first step toward making natural, wholesome soaps for you and your family.

Why soap making is a natural choice for a healthy lifestyle

I'm betting that, like me, what is most important to you is ensuring a healthy lifestyle for you and your family. That's what drew me to soap making – the knowledge that I would be able to produce a natural, more environmentally sound soap for me and my family. It gave me peace of mind to know I would be able to control exactly what goes into my soap and how much fragrance it does or doesn't have and knowing I'd be able to control the costs. Now, I can make spa-quality soaps in my own kitchen for a fraction of what those boutiques at the mall charge (and you don't need an advanced biochemistry degree to read the ingredients list of my bar).

Plus, I wound up having lot of fun!

Frankly, one key factor that makes homemade soap so attractive today is being able to avoid all the dyes and chemicals, primarily stabilizers, pH balancers, etc., the commercial soap industry put in their products.

I picked up a bar of facial cleansing soap at the drug store the other day and looked at the list of ingredients. Triethanolamine, TEA stearate, sodium tallowate…wow. What a list. Let's just tackle that first one.

> Also available in Original and Acne-Prone Skin formulas.
> **Ingredients:** Triethanolamine, TEA Stearate, Sodium Tallowate, Glycerin, Water, Sodium Cocoate, Sodium Ricinoleate, Sodium Oleate, Cocamide MEA, Sodium Stearate, BHT, Tocopheryl Acetate, Tetrasodium Etidronate, Trisodium HEDTA, Disodium Cocoamphodiacetate (1347-016)
> Questions or comments? 1-800-

Study: Ingredient in Commercial Soap Causes Cancer in Mice

Triethanolamine, also known as TEA, is a pH balancer used in many cosmetics. According to a 2004 study, it was also shown to cause liver cancer in mice. I can't think of a better reason to make your own soap for you and your family.

To be fair, sodium tallowate and sodium stearate are fancy ways of saying fat that has been turned into soap with lye – this is the saponification process. I'll explain that process in a later chapter, and believe me when I say that lye isn't as scary as you might think. However, some of the other chemicals and stabilizers commercial soap producers use are just not necessary and you won't be using them to make soap in your own kitchen.

And let's address fragrance. Some of us, I'm including myself in the "us" pack, are sensitive to strong scents. When I shop at the mall, I have to navigate waaay around the fragrance counter at the department stores. I enjoy very lightly scented soaps, so that's what I make for myself.

You can also make soaps that enliven your senses with fragrances. Check out the entire chapter I've devoted to fragrance and be sure to read the section on combining scent combinations and how to test fragrance pairings to create your own harmonious aromatherapy spa right in one bar of soap.

And it's really not as difficult as you might think. What if I told you, that you could make soap in less time that it takes to make soup and you can do it using the same appliance – your crock pot! That's my preferred method. It's pretty quick and easy, plus, I get to use my soap almost immediately. (I'm not always very patient.)

But let's go over all the different ways to make soap. I'll walk you through it, step by step.

Chapter 2 – How Do I Do It?

You know that you want to control the ingredients in your family's soap; you want to create natural, wholesome bars of spa-quality soap that will leave your skin feeling refreshed, revitalized and youthful.

Now we need to determine which method of soap making is right for you. Let's look at the four methods of making homemade soap.

4 Methods of Soap Making & Deciding Which is Best for You

1. **Melt and Pour** – This is the Quick Start Way. Read this section of this book and you'll have a bar of your own handcrafted soap in your hands tonight. As the name suggests, this involves melting a block of "base" soap purchased from a wholesaler or craft store. You can add skin-safe fragrance and dye.
2. **Cold Process** – Most soap makers use this method. This involves making soap "from scratch" using a recipe that contains a balanced ratio of oils (fats) and lye, along with water.

3. **Hot Process** – This is another "from scratch" method using a carefully balanced ratio of oils and lye, but this mixture is cooked on the stovetop or in a crockpot.
4. **Rebatching** – Shaving, grating or grinding bars of soap and melting them down using water or milk to reblend them into a new concoction.

Deciding which method is best for you might be a matter of trial and error. You might want to test out various methods to see which you prefer. I started with a few Melt and Pour (M&P) batches when I began because I wasn't sure if I wanted to invest a lot of money into something I might not like. Well, I knew after my first batch, I'd love it, so I graduated upward and finally decided that the crockpot Hot Process (HP) method is my favorite. But don't let me influence you. I know some "soapers" (the affectionate term for those of us who love to make soap) who swear by the cold process (CP) method and won't switch. Read through the step-by-step instructions for each of the methods in later chapters and you might find yourself gravitating toward one more than another.

I would still suggest you might start with the M&P method, just to get your feet wet and to get a feel for pouring the molds, handling fragrances, dyes, etc. The M&P method is an excellent training ground for the CP and HP methods. But starting with CP or HP or even rebatching is okay, too. Let your interests guide you. You want to wind up with soaps you and your family will enjoy, but you should also enjoy the process of making them.

The Tools of the Trade are Probably Already in Your Kitchen

You're probably wondering what kind of equipment you'll need to get started. Well, if you take the Quick Start Way, you'll just need to make a trip to local craft store for few things and you can have a bar of soap ready to use before bedtime. Seriously.

If you want to get serious about making all-natural, made from scratch homemade soaps, you'll likely need to order a few ingredients from a wholesale supplier, but the good news is that you likely have most of the basic equipment you'll need right in your own kitchen.

Here's the list of essential equipment you'll need for the CP and HP methods of soap making:

- **A digital scale.** Some recipes call for measures down to $1/10^{th}$ of an ounce, so a digital scale is essential. To be successful at soap making, you have to measure everything exactly.

- **A 2-3 quart heat-resistant heavy plastic pitcher with lid** for mixing your lye and solution (you can also use stainless steel, but I prefer plastic). Be sure to label this: "danger lye" and don't use it for any other purpose.

- **A plastic spoon** for stirring the lye solution (be sure never to use an aluminum, tin or copper spoon, as these metals react with the lye).

- **An 8-12 quart stainless steel pot with lid.** This is your "soap pot" that you'll use to your melt oils and blending the soap. Again, you want to make sure the pot is stainless steel. You may also use enameled steel, but those can be pricy. If you don't have a spare stainless steel pot, restaurant supply stores have great prices on large pots like this.

- **A 2-3 quart plastic or glass pitcher (Pyrex works very well) or a large bowl** to measure and set aside your oils before you add them to the soap pot.

- **An accurate thermometer** (preferably digital) to monitor the lye solution and the melted oils temperatures.

- **Safety goggles and rubber gloves** to protect your eyes and hands from the lye solution.
- **Stainless steel measuring spoons** for fragrance or essential oils, skin-safe dyes and/or additives (dried lavender leaves, etc.).
- **Several small bowls, ramekins or measuring cups** to hold the additives, fragrances, essential oils, skin-safe dyes, etc., that you've measured out before adding them to your batch of soap.
- **A large stainless steel or heat-resistant plastic ladle**.
- **A few heat-resistant spatulas.**
- **An immersion ("stick") blender** to thoroughly mix the oils and lye solution to complete the saponification (soap making) process.

- **A soap mold** to pour your soap into until it sets and hardens. You can buy a commercially made mold (there's a huge variety available made of silicone and plastic created to mimic a wide number of soap shapes and designs).

I enjoy cooking, so my kitchen is pretty well equipped, so I had most of these items. I did need to purchase a digital scale, however, and I bought plastic utensils that I labeled "soap" with an indelible marker and I keep those with my soap making supplies so I don't use them for cooking.

Tip: Thrift stores are good places to shop for these supplies.

A few notes about soap molds: Craft and wholesalers offer so many choices of soap molds, that you can create everything from delicate guest soaps to all kinds of whimsical shapes. However, the silicone molds, while absolutely dream-like to unmold your bars of soap, can be pricey for a beginner. Each one is about $15 to $25, depending upon the size (as of this writing). Plastic molds are less expensive, but can crack with repeated use if you're not very careful.

You don't have to spend a fortune to get started, however. Check eBay and Craigslist for used soap molds.

DIY soap molds

You can make your own soap mold from virtually any leak-proof container either made

Virtually anything can be turned into a soap mold – even a well-washed potato chip can.

from plastic, glass or stainless steel or even wood and cardboard if the container is first lined with freezer paper. You can even use a bread loaf pan, but be sure you DO NOT use it to bake bread again. Store it with your soap making equipment to ensure you don't get it mixed up with your bake ware.

If you Google "DIY wooden soap loaf mold," you'll also find tons of plans and easy-to-follow instructions for building what amounts to a simple rectangular box for pouring your soap.

Making soap in a loaf mold allows you to have a lot of latitude for creativity.

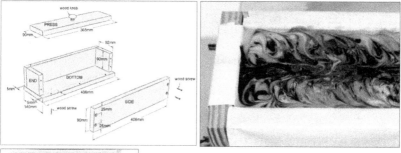

If you build a simple rectangular loaf mold (Google DIY plans), you can separate your next batch of soap, create complementary colors or even scents, and then pour them into your mold and swirl them together before the soap sets (above). Break open the mold, cut the soap loaf into bars the end result will be gorgeous, unique bars of spa-quality soap.

Melt and Pour: Quick Start Way – Let's Make Soap TODAY!

If you're as excited about soap making as I was when I first made up my mind to do it, you want to get started right away. With a quick trip to your local craft or discount store, you can get started today. However, if you want to get really serious about creating natural, wholesome soap, even vegan soaps, for you and your family, read on.

The fastest way to make soap is the "Melt and Pour" (M&P) method. Craft and discount stores, as well as online soap supply wholesalers sell blocks of soap base in several varieties: glycerin (semi-translucent and clear), white, goat milk, aloe vera, etc.

These bases are unscented and once melted down, you can add cosmetic grade (approved by the Food and Drug Administration (FDA) to be used on the skin) fragrance oils and dyes.

Step One – Purchase the soap base of your choice from the craft or discount store, along with any skin-safe fragrance and color, plus some soap molds/trays. You can find a kit for about $20 at your local craft store that will give you just enough "stuff" to make about 10 little bars, complete with fragrance and dye. You'll also get step-by-step instructions, but I'm still going to walk you through it!

Step Two – Carefully cut several small chunks off the block of the soap base and place them in a double boiler or in a microwave-safe bowl covered in plastic wrap (I prefer a double boiler). If you don't have a double boiler, you can make one by using a large saucepan with about an inch and a half of boiling water and then placing a metal bowl or a smaller saucepan over the top of the large pan, being careful of the steam. Caution: The soap base gets very hot when it melts completely.

Step Three – Add any coloring or fragrance to the melted base. If you want to do multiple colors for a layered look, now is the time to split your melted base into two vessels. Pyrex measuring pitchers work well as they let you ensure you have equal parts in each one.

Step Four – Pour the base into your molds. And…wait. As soon as it cools and hardens, the bar of soap should pop right out of the mold. Melt and Pour bases do not need time to cure or harden like cold process or hot process method soaps, so it's fine to go ahead and use your M&P soap right away.

The creative possibilities for melt and pour soaps are almost limitless. For beginners, trying out new scent combinations with a melt and pour base is a great way to flex our creative muscles right from the start.

Lavender is a great starting point for almost any scent combo, lavender-vanilla, lavender-lemongrass, lavender-orange, the list goes on and on! Add in some dried lavender and a purple ribbon and you've got a gift for any occasion – birthday, housewarming, wedding shower, you name it.

Pros and Cons of M&P Soap: The great thing about M&P soap is that you can start "soaping" right away. You don't have to make a major investment and the soap is ready to use right away. The not-so-great thing about M&P is that, sort of like commercial soap, you don't have control over the ingredients. What you're making is only as good as your base and sometimes the base you find at craft stores is not high quality. The manufacturers often add chemicals to boost lather or to help the base melt faster.

Chapter 3 – Safety First

The truth about lye

The truth is lye demands your respect, but there is no more reason to fear it than you might fear your gas stove or any other potentially dangerous item in your kitchen.

As long as you are careful with lye and remember one simple rule: always add lye on top of your measured amount of water to avoid a possible volcanic reaction from the lye. Also, when mixing the lye solution, do not stand directly over the vessel and breathe the fumes that might rise directly up from the solution. It's a good idea to turn on your stove's exhaust fan to clear the kitchen of any possible fumes.

Safety equipment you must have

- **Safety goggles/glasses and rubber/latex gloves** to protect your eyes and hands from the lye solution as I mentioned in the list of equipment in Chapter 2.
- **Common sense.** Use your best judgement and be careful.

We all know that the kitchen is the most dangerous room in our home, therefore, we should exercise extra caution when we work around the big machines that make fire and we should be careful when we use all the sharp pointy things that we keep in those drawers and cabinets. Simple, right?

I'm not making light of this. You really should be careful. Vinegar is a neutralizer for lye, so keep an open bottle of vinegar on hand when making lye soap, just in case any spills happen.

Making lye soap really isn't much more dangerous than fileting a fish or searing a steak. You just have to pay attention to what you're doing. However, you wouldn't let your 5-year-old clean a trout or grill a T-bone, so don't let your kids help mix the lye solution while you're making soap. Let them help you wrap the bars up for gifts, but keep them out of the kitchen during the processing time.

Chapter 4 – Starting From Scratch
Our First Batch of Natural Soap

Step-by-step guide for cold process soap making

Making cold process soap is no more complicated than following a recipe for baking a cake. Less complicated really, because you don't have to worry about baking anything.

You just need to ensure that you measure everything correctly and heat all the oils called for in your recipe in your soap pot until they reach about 100 degrees. Next, you slowly add a mixture of water and lye (that you've also carefully measured) and blend it together with an immersion ("stick") blender until it thickens, add skin-safe color and fragrance, and then pour it in molds. You'll have hardened, but still "raw" soap in 24 hours, but at this point you may cut it into bars and set it aside to harden and cure for about four weeks. Then it's spa time!

Now let's take it from the top…

Step 1 – Get organized and prepare your ingredients, including the lye

Get all your equipment out, organized and ready to use. You don't want to start fumbling for a measuring cup in the middle of this process. Also, banish all children, animals and other distractions from your kitchen and put away any food you might have on the stove. You don't want to get any soap in the soup or vice versa.

Get a printout of your recipe or ensure you have it up on your computer screen, iPad, etc. I prefer a hard copy because I don't want to take a chance on getting my electronic devices wet, plus, if you're wearing latex gloves, you're going to have a tough time with tough screens.

Measure out all your ingredients. This is why it's handy to have a number of small glass or plastic bowls/cups.

Next, carefully prepare your lye mixture. This is the time for your gloves and safety eyewear. Remember, lye shouldn't be feared, but it should be respected, much like a sharp knife in your kitchen, you need to take precautions when using both.

It's also a good idea to place your pitcher of measured water on your range/stovetop with the hood vent turned on before you do this so the vent can help dissipate any fumes that might rise from the mixture. Remember to always add the lye to the water instead of the other way around or you might end up with a nasty volcanic reaction.

Stir the lye solution, taking care not to put your face directly over the container nor to breathe in the fumes. This lye solution will be hot. Set it aside to cool off for a bit.

While the lye cools, you can prepare your soap mold(s). If you're using a loaf mold, you can line it with freezer paper. Or if you're using a plastic or silicone mold and you prefer it, you might want to spray your mold with "release spray" to make it easier to pop the bars out later. Whatever you choose to use, you'll want to have something ready to pour your raw soap into as soon as it's ready, so it helps to do as much preparation on the front end of this project as possible.

Step 2 – Weigh your oils

Decide which vessel you'll use to pour your soap making oils and place that on your digital scale. For example, you might use a glass Pyrex-type pitcher. Now zero out your digital scale. This will ensure the scale isn't weighing the pitcher along with your oils, which would, of course, through off your calculations.

Step 3 – Heat your solid oils and mix with the liquid oils

Your recipe will likely call for some "solid" oils like coconut oil or palm oil or cocoa butter. Place these carefully measured solid oils in your soap making aluminum pot (remember that other metals react with lye) and melt the oils. The melting point should be about 100 degrees. Next, add the rest of your oils and bring the entire mixture up to 100 degrees and remove from heat.

Check the temperature of your lye mixture. As a rule of thumb, your oils and lye mixture should be roughly the same temperature. If your oils get too hot, the whole mixture is likely to bubble over. This is especially true of the HP method when you're "cooking" your mixture over a longer period of time. You really don't want a big mess of raw soap oozing all over your kitchen, so tend to the temperature closely.

Step 4 – Let the saponification begin!

It's time to add the lye mixture, which means it's time to really make soap! Saponification is a process that produces soap from fats and lye.

Plug in your immersion ("stick") blender and get the lye mixture. You'll also want to have your pre-measured skin-safe fragrance oils and colorants nearby. Things are going to start taking shape before you know it.

Slowly, pour in the lye mixture. The oil will immediately turn cloudy. This is normal. Insert your stick blender into the oil mixture and start stirring it, but don't turn it on yet, just stir. Now, start turning on the stick blender in short pulses of about five seconds or so, while continuing to stir the mixture.

The mixture will begin to thicken. Keep pulsing at longer intervals with the blender as it thickens and eventually just keep the blender on once you feel the consistency is that of a thick soup. Be sure to move the blender all around the pot and through the mixture from top to bottom.

Once your soap (yes, it is soap now) starts looking like a custard, turn off the blender and let some of the soap drop on the surface of the pot. If the droplets remain and are visible for several seconds without immediately smoothing back under the surface, you've reached the stage known as "trace." This can also be seen by dragging a spoon or the blender across the surface and a line or "trace" should be visible. I find the droplets easier to see than the line. You should reach trace within 15 minutes or less, depending on your recipe. Stick blenders have made soap making much faster than previously when soap makers had to stir and stir and stir to reach trace. Thank goodness for modern conveniences!

Step 5 – Add fragrance and colorant

We're just about there. If you've decided to create a duo-color soap, now is the time to separate your batch into two parts and color each separately. If you want them both to have the same scent, add the fragrance first. If you want to just have a simple one-color, one-fragrance soap, and then simply stir in your skin-safe colorant and fragrance oil. Blend well.

Now is also the time for any additives you might choose to enhance the rejuvenating properties of your soap. For example, you might choose to sprinkle in exfoliates, such as oat scrub or botanicals, like lavender buds.

Step 6 – Pour the soap in your mold

This is the only step that I usually ask someone to lend a hand doing, since it's one that must be done quickly and it can get a bit messy since you're wielding a big soap pot.

Hopefully, you've prepped your soap molds and have them set aside and ready to go. I usually have someone steady the molds while I pour the soap or vice versa.

Use a spatula to scrape out your pot and to spread the soap evenly in the molds. If you've ever baked a cake, this method will sound familiar – whack the molds. That's right, whack 'em. What I really mean is pick them up a couple inches from the surface of the table and drop them back down to release the trapped bubbles. You want a nice, solid bar of soap, not a hole-filled one, so whack it!

Cover the molds with plastic wrap and then drape them with an old beach or bath towel to keep them warm. This helps speed the saponification of the soap.

Wash up! Put on your gloves (the soap you made is still in its "raw" state and will be harsh on your skin) and wash everything. When putting away the measuring cups and pitchers, be sure not to mix up anything used with lye with any of your everyday kitchenware.

Step 7 – Set it aside – Cold process soap will harden enough to cut into bars (or remove from molds) within 24 hours. In fact, it's easier to cut at this point when it's a bit softer. However, it is not safe to use yet. The lye is still too caustic and harsh for your skin. The saponification process is still happening and will continue for the next 3 to 4 weeks.

So once you've cut the soap into bars, place the bars on wax paper or brown paper and space them apart so air can circulate between them. Place them in a large cardboard box and set the box aside in a well-ventilated area.

Chapter 5 – This is Not Your Granny's Lye Soap

Hot Process (HP) soap might sound like a labour-intensive, steamy way of going about making soap, but in reality, it's just a way to speed saponification (turning lye and fats into soap) through the application of heat during the soap-making process. I like it because I'm a bit impatient about wanting to use my soaps sooner, rather than later and HP soaps don't have the long curing time that CP soaps do. And I finally have a great use for my crock pot!

Most of the steps are the same as the CP soap making method.

Step-by-step guide for hot process (HP) soap making

Step 1 – Get organized and prepare your ingredients, including the lye (see CP method)

Step 2 – Weigh your oils (see CP method)

Step 3 – Heat your solid oils and mix with the liquid oils – Here's where we deviate from the CP method. Place your carefully weighed oils in your soap making pot on the stovetop or in a crockpot (my preferred method) and turn the heat on low-medium. Monitor the temperature and ensure the oils do not exceed 150 degrees. Remove the oils from the heat once the temp is between 120 and 160 degrees. If you're using a crock pot that allows you to remove the inner "crock" do this to remove the oil mixture from the heating elements. Remember to check the temperature of your lye mixture. You're aiming for an oil mixture and lye mixture temp within about 20 degrees of one another.

Step 4 – Let the saponification begin! – (see CP method)

Step 5 – Time to cook the soap – Once you've reached the "trace" stage, you'll need to cook your batch of soap to let the saponification continue. If you're using a crock pot, return the crock to the heating element, turn it on "high" and be sure to put the lid on securely. If you're cooking on the stovetop, use a low heat setting and cover the pot. You want your soap to cook at about 200 degrees, so you might need to keep checking the temp to ensure you have the right setting on your heating element. This is why I like the crock pot. High on a crock pot is about 200 degrees.

The batch will take about 2 to 3 hours to cook, depending on the kinds of oils used in your recipe. Keep an eye on it and stir it about every 20 minutes.

Your soap will go through **three stages**. Each stage will make you think you've got a disaster on your hands. Don't worry! Be patient. Your soap will turn out beautifully in the end.

> **Stage 1:** Separation – The soap may look like it's falling to pieces with the solids and liquids going in different directions. Hang in there, give it a stir, and wait for stage 2.
>
> **Stage 2:** Rejoining and Rising: Before you know it, your soap will come together and start rising like bread dough. In fact, it might rise so much you'll get a bit worried. Just stir it slowly and it will settle down a bit. You don't want it to overflow, so keep a close eye on it during this stage and keep stirring it slowly. You may need to reduce the heat a bit if you're using the stovetop method.
>
> **Stage 3:** Oily Mashed Potatoes: You're almost there! It doesn't look like something you want to eat, but it is soap, after all. Once you start seeing a gloss and see fewer and fewer bubbles, you'll know the batch has

finished saponifying. If you want to, you could test the pH at this point (ideally, you want a pH of 8-10).

Step 5 – Add fragrance and colorant – This step is the same as with the CP method, but HP soap is much, much thicker, so stirring in the additives can be tougher. Think of stirring oatmeal into thick mashed potatoes. That's a bit what it's like.

Step 6 – Pour the soap in your mold – Again, this is the same as with the CP method, but the HP soap is very thick, so it's more like spreading it into a mold sometimes rather than pouring it, depending on the recipe.

Step 7 – Set it aside – Unlike the CP method, you only need to let your HP soap cure a short time. Some soap makers suggest letting it cure for a week or two weeks before using it to ensure it's not too harsh for the skin, however, if the soap has hardened enough, it should be perfectly okay to use 24 to 48 hours after you make it. That's the point of "cooking" it – to speed the saponification. Of course, it melts faster in water if it hasn't fully hardened, so if you have a recipe for a very creamy body bar, you might want to give it a week to harden before using it.

Note: Any cold process (CP) soap recipe can be modified as outlined above and turned into a hot process (HP) method recipe.

Chapter 6 – Recipes
Soaps That Will Revitalize Your Skin

Soap making is alchemy and a bit of culinary creativity combined. These recipes will give you the framework to inspire your imagination after learning the techniques explained in this book. But you might want to eventually try your hand at creating your own recipes. Or you might find a recipe you sort of like, but perhaps you want to modify it or add an ingredient you're particularly fond of, like coconut oil. You can do that, but always use saponification or lye calculator first.

Use an online lye calculator

The main thing you want to keep in mind is to ensure your ratios of water, oil and lye are correct in your recipe. The easiest way to do this is by using an online lye calculator. A Google search will turn up dozens and there's even software available for purchase to help you calculate your recipes.

The Handcrafted Soap & Cosmetic Guild is an international non-profit trade association that promotes the benefits of handcrafted soaps and cosmetics. They have a free lye calculator on their website that is easy to use.

http://www.soapguild.org/soapmakers/resources/lye-calc.php

Once you plug in your ingredients (I suggest you start with a basic recipe you like and modify it) to the calculator, you'll get a readout with a percentage next to the lye amount and a suggested amount for the water in your recipe. The percentage is the excess fat range.

What does the online lye calculator reading mean?

When calculating a new recipe, I follow this rule of thumb:

- **0% to 4% excess fat range:** DANGER ZONE! Time to go back and redo my ratios of lye vs. fats/oils. Any soap with this much lye content will be harsh and dangerous to the skin. It might also present problems in manufacturing.

- **5% to 8% excess fat range:** Comfort zone. This is my usual target.

- **9% to 10% excess fat range:** Bordering on too soft. Depending on the types of fats used in the recipe, this range can be a bit too soft and sticky.

Cold Process Recipes

This is a wonderful recipe, used with permission, courtesy of © Rebecca's Soap Delicatessen.

It's one that will suit both men and women, but because the activated charcoal turns the soap black, it gives it a rather "manly" appeal. The lavender and tea tree oil imbue this soap with a light, fresh scent. The tea tree oil leaves the skin feeling just a bit tingly, while the combination of oils makes this a well-balanced moisturizing bar. Meanwhile, the activated charcoal helps draw out skin impurities, which makes this an ideal recipe for anyone looking for an acne prevention soap. Tea tree oil is considered antibacterial, which lends itself to acne prevention, and lavender sooths and calms irritated skin.

Activated Charcoal Lavender & Tea Tree Cold Process Soap Recipe

© 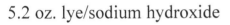 Rebecca's Soap Delicatessen

Ingredients

10.8 oz. hemp seed oil

7.2 oz. palm kernel flakes

9 oz. 76°F melt point coconut oil

7.2 oz. macadamia nut oil

1.8 oz. shea butter

5.2 oz. lye/sodium hydroxide

11.5 oz. distilled water

.72 oz. lavender essential oil

.36 oz. tea tree oil

2 Tablespoons activated charcoal

Instructions:

This is a cold process soap recipe therefore to create this soap recipe you'll need to follow your basic cold process soap making instructions and remember to take all safety precautions.

Using a digital scale, begin by weighing out the water and lye separately, then pour the lye slowly into the distilled water and mix until all of the lye has dissolved. Set aside to cool.

Now prepare your soap making oils by weighing them out and combining in a large stainless steel pot. Heat on the stove over medium heat until all oils have melted then remove from heat and allow to cool.

Once the lye-water and oils have cool to about 100-degree mix the lye-water and oils together using a stick blender. At light trace, add the essential oils and activated charcoal and mix completely, then prepare into your prepared soap mold. Cover and insulate for 24 hours. Allow to cure 3-6 weeks before use, then wrap and label as desired.

Luxuriating Body Bar

This is a silky, smooth, moisturizing body bar, great for all skin types. It molds beautifully, so if you're ready to try a fancy floral or exotic-shaped mold, this would be a great recipe to use.

Ingredients:

3 oz. Avocado Oil

2 oz. Castor Oil,

3 oz. Jojoba Oil

12 oz. Olive Oil

6 oz. Palm Oil

5 oz. Palm Kernel Oil

1 oz. Wheat Germ Oil

1 oz. Beeswax

4.1 oz. Lye

10 oz. Cold Water

Instructions:

Follow basic CP methods. This recipe traces quickly, so add any fragrance oils and/or essential oils at light trace. Pour into molds (and by the way, it's a great recipe if you want to use fancy molds) and cover lightly for about 24 hours.

Hot Process Recipes

Follow the step-by-step guide to hot process soap making for detailed directions.

This is a "version" of castile-like soap. It's not a true castile soap because it's not 100% olive oil, but soaps made with 100% olive oil take a long time to bring to trace and can be very hard bars or soap. This one is a bit more balanced and yet is still very moisturizing.

Crockpot Castile Soap

- 26 oz. olive oil
- 26 oz. coconut oil
- 2 oz. castor oil
- 8.38 oz. lye
- 20 oz. distilled water

This soap takes about two hours to "cook" completely.

The above recipe is a great "base" for a variety of revitalizing, refreshing recipes.

Rosemary-Mint Castile Crockpot Soap

At the "trace" stage of the crockpot castile soap, add:

- 3 Tbsp. dried and crushed rosemary leaves
- ½ oz. Peppermint Essential Oil
- ½ oz. Rosemary Essential Oil

Orange-Eucalyptus Castile Crockpot Soap

- ½ oz. Sweet Orange Essential oil
- ¼ oz. Eucalyptus Essential oil
- ½ oz. Citronella oil

Chapter 7 – Sweet Smell of Success

One of the great things about making your own soaps is that your soaps will not only be natural and revitalizing to your skin, but you can also make wonderful aroma therapy soaps to create the full spa experience right at home. A word of caution: Always, always, always use skin-safe, cosmetic-grade fragrance/essential oils.

When you begin thinking about blending fragrances, think about combinations you already like and why they are complementary. Most successful fragrance combinations have three elements:

Top Note: These are fresh, intense fragrances that are stimulating and energizing. Examples are Bergamot, Orange, Lemongrass, Pine, Eucalyptus and Peppermint.

Middle Note: These are strong scents that tend to develop after the top note dissipates, however the middle note is usually longer lasting. Examples are Lavender, Rosemary, Tea Tree, Chamomile, Juniper and Nutmeg.

Base Note: These are the heaviest of the three elements of scents. The base note takes longer to reach the senses, but tends to lingers longer than the other two notes, which gives the fragrance staying power. Examples are Patchouli, Sandalwood, Clove, Rose, Jasmine and Cedarwood.

How to Test Fragrance Combinations

Before trying out a new fragrance combination you're sure will work "in theory" and whipping up a new batch of soap with your fragrance idea, it's best to do a bit of testing.
For this test, you'll need the fragrance oils you plan to combine, a few clean cotton swabs and a clean glass jar or other glass container with an airtight lid large enough to hold the swabs.

1. Open the jars/bottles of the fragrance oils you plan to use for your fragrance combo. Having the fragrance permeate the air will give you a bit of a preview of the blended scent.

2. Touch just the tip of a cotton swab on the surface of the oil of the first fragrance. Drop the swab into the clean glass container.

3. Repeat this process with the remaining fragrances using a new, clean cotton swab for each new fragrance.

4. Close the glass container with the cotton swabs inside and leave it alone for half an hour or more. Sure to close

up the bottles/jars of your fragrance oils and put them away.

5. If the air in the room still smells like your fragrance oils, take the container with the cotton swabs to another room and to "cleanse the palate" of your senses, smell coffee beans before opening the container to smell the cotton swabs with your test fragrance blend.

6. You might want to leave the container closed in a cool, dark place for a few hours and return to try the scent again after the scents have "married" a bit. It could take about 48 hours for the scent to mature and all the notes to blend.

7. Be sure to write down your observations. You might want to make corrections. Perhaps go back and add two cotton swabs (two parts) of one particular fragrance over another. Experiment and have fun!

Essential Oil Combinations that Work

Here are some scent combinations that just naturally go together. They're harmonious with the top, middle and base notes blending well to create a well-rounded fragrance.

Think about some of the colognes you've enjoyed over the years and try to identify the aromas – the notes – present in those fragrances and pinpoint why you enjoyed the scents so much. This might help you in coming up with your own fragrances.

- Lemongrass – Lavender – Basil
- Apple – Vanilla – Cinnamon
- Lemon – Rosemary – Cedar

Most importantly, your nose knows what you like. Try the scent test with the fragrance combinations and decide what enlivens your senses. Just be sure to cleanse your palate with a whiff of coffee beans between fragrance combos or you'll overwhelm your sense of smell.

Chapter 8 – Resources

Getting Down to Business

Thinking of making a business of your new soap making hobby? Here are some helpful links:

- The Food and Drug Administration has an FAQ on laws pertaining to the manufacture and sale of homemade soaps.

- The Handcrafted Soap and Cosmetic Guild is a non-profit trade association that is actively involved in education, promotion and legislative advocacy for the handcrafted soap and cosmetic industry as a whole.

- The National Association of Women Business Owners is the only dues-based organization representing the interests of all women entrepreneurs across all industries; and boasts 60 chapters across the country.

Talking With Fellow "Soapers"

One of the greatest resources you'll find as you navigate through your first few batches of all-natural soap, is the advice of more experienced soap maker ("soaper" as we sometimes call ourselves). Take a moment to Google "soap making message boards" and you'll turn up dozens of results, if not hundreds.

Your local craft store may conduct soap making classes, so you might be able to connect with the instructor if you have a specific question about a recipe or fragrance combination or simply want to talk about the joy of soap making with someone who understands why it's so important to you.

Don't overlook social media. Pinterest, Yahoo Groups and Facebook are loaded with topics devoted to all the finer points of soap making, along with hundreds of fabulous botanical recipes. You're not  alone! There are tons of people out there just like you and I who want to create wholesome, natural, revitalizing soaps. Talk to fellow soap makers at the next craft show or fair you attend. You'll find a wealth of information from others who are just as interested in the craft and who are eager to share what they've learned along the way. Don't be shy!

Now, thanks to the techniques you've learned in this book and the recipes you have to get you started, you are well on your way to creating spa-quality soaps to enrich your skin, revitalize your senses and relax your body. Congratulations!

www.ingramcontent.com/pod-product-compliance
Lightning Source LLC
LaVergne TN
LVHW012257220225
804335LV00009B/928